D1489515

PICTURE A COUNTRY

Australia

Henry Pluckrose

WELLS PUBLIC LIBRARY
54 1st STREET S.W.
WELLS, MN 56097

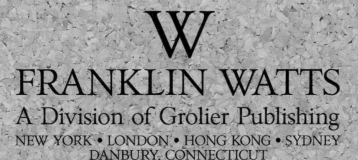

W

FRANKLIN WATTS

A Division of Grolier Publishing

NEW YORK • LONDON • HONG KONG • SYDNEY
DANBURY, CONNECTICUT

This is the Australian flag.

Photographic acknowledgements:

Cover: Top right, Eye Ubiquitous (Grenville Turner/Wildlight Photo Agency), bottom left, Robert Harding Picture Library (D. Jacobs), bottom right (above), Bruce Coleman (Fritz Prenzel), bottom right (below), Window on the World (David Usill).

AA Photo Library p. 22, 23t, 23b; Bruce Coleman Collection pp. 8, 18 (Fritz Prenzel), 17b (Dr. Frieder Sauer); Colorific pp 12-13 (Bill Bachman), 16 (Patrick Ward), 20 (Penny Tweedie), 27 (Roger Garwood); James Davis Travel Photography p. 15; Eye Ubiquitous pp. 8-9 (Tony Brow Photography), 21 (Grenville Turner/Wildlight Photography), 28 (Paul Thompson); Getty Images p. 13 (Trevor Mein); Ronald Grant Archive p. 25b; Robert Harding Picture Library pp. 14 (D. Jacobs), 26 (Robert Francis), 29t; Image Bank p. 29b; Images Colour Library p.10; Impact Photos pp. 19 (Tom Webster), 24 (Neil Morrison); Christine Osborne Photos p. 25t; Spectrum Colour Library pp. 10-11; Window on the World Photo Library p. 17t (David Ustill).

All other photography Steve Shott.
Map by Julian Baker.

Series editor: Rachel Cooke
Series designer: Kirstie Billingham
Editor: Alex Young
Picture research: Sue Mennell

First published in 1999 by Franklin Watts
First American edition 1999 by
Franklin Watts
A division of Grolier Publishing
90 Sherman Turnpike
Danbury, CT 06816

Visit Franklin Watts on the Internet at:
http://publishing.grolier.com

Pluckrose, Henry Arthur.
    Australia / Henry Pluckrose.
        p. cm. -- (Picture a country)
    Includes index.
    Summary: A simple introduction to the landscape, people, cities, industries, culture, and animals of Australia.
    ISBN 0-531-14510 7
    1. Australia --Juvenile literature. [1. Australia.] I. Title.
II. Series: Pluckrose, Henry Arthur. Picture a country.
DU96.P57 1999
994--dc21   98-30778
                                                            CIP
                                                             AC

GROLIER
PUBLISHING

Copyright © Franklin Watts 1999
Printed in Great Britain

Junior
994
Pluckro
E.t

Contents

#34739612 1PL7
11·18·99

Where Is Australia?

This is a map of Australia. Australia is a huge island south of Asia, in the Southern Hemisphere. Tasmania, a smaller island to the southeast of the mainland, is also part of Australia.

Here are some Australian stamps and money.

Australian money is counted in dollars.

Pacific Ocean

Indonesia

New Guinea

Coral Sea

Darwin

Indian Ocean

Great Barrier Reef

Northern Territory

Queensland

Australia

Alice Springs

▲
Uluru

Western Australia

South Australia

Brisbane ●

New South Wales

Blue Mountains
▲
Broken Hill ●
Sydney ●

Perth ●

Canberra
(ACT)

Adelaide ●

Victoria

Melbourne ●

Tasmania

Hobart ●

Southern Ocean

The Australian Landscape

Australia has many kinds of landscape. There are mountain ranges, tropical rain forests, and green plains. But most of Australia is dry desert and scrub land, which stretches for many thousands of miles.

The desert regions of Australia are known as the Outback.

The peaks of the Three Sisters range are in the Blue Mountains in New South Wales.

Because Australia is in the Southern Hemisphere, its seasons are in the opposite order to countries north of the equator. Summer is from December to February and winter from June to August.

The Australian People

The Aborigines are the native people of Australia. They first came to Australia over 40,000 years ago from islands in the Indian and Pacific oceans.

When British people came to Australia in the 18th century, many Aborigines were forced to leave their land.

Crowds gather to watch the famous Melbourne Cup horse race.

More than 18 million people live in Australia today. They have come from more than 200 different countries, including Great Britain, Ireland, Italy, and several Asian countries.

The city of Hobart in Tasmania.

Where They Live

Most Australians live in towns and cities along the south and east coasts, where the weather is rarely too hot or too cold. There are also many small towns in the Outback.

Nearly 3 million people live in Melbourne.

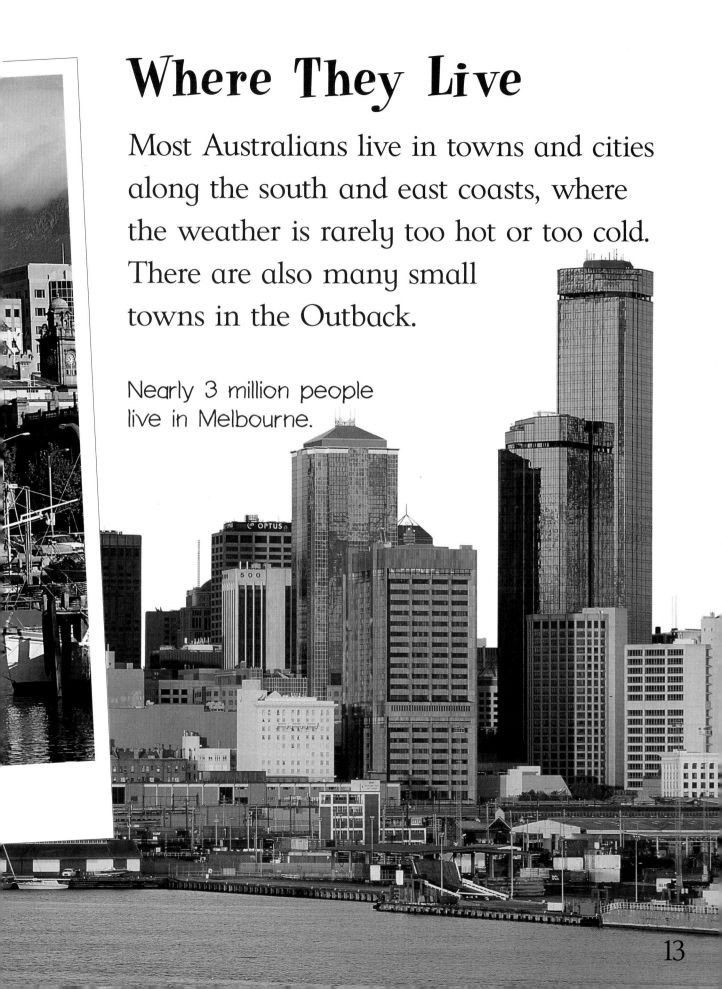

Capital Cities

Australia is divided into different states and territories, each with its own capital. The state capitals are: Sydney (New South Wales) Adelaide (South Australia), Brisbane (Queensland), Perth (Western Australia), Melbourne (Victoria), and Hobart (Tasmania).

Sydney's Opera House is one of the most famous sights in Australia.

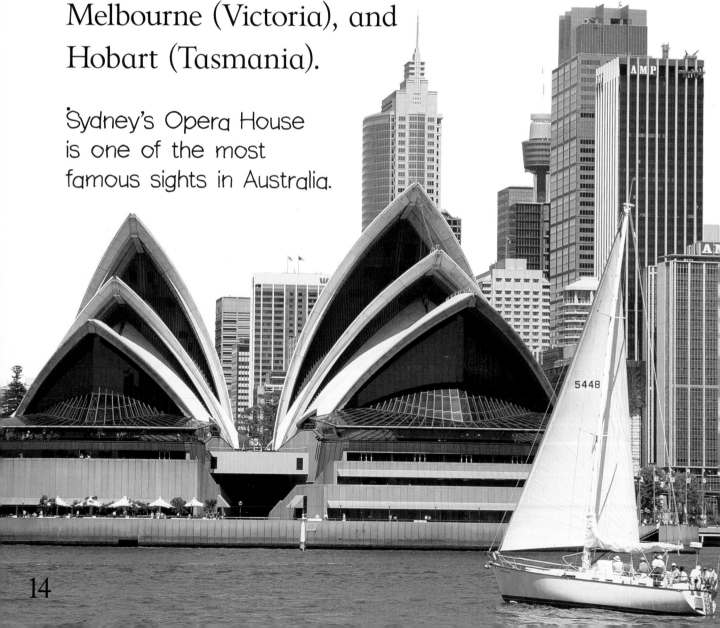

Canberra, in the Australian Capital Territory (ACT), is the capital of all of Australia. The most important building in the city is the Parliament Building.

Diamonds and Opals

Mining is important in Australia.
Its rocks contain many precious stones,
such as diamonds and opals. There are
also valuable metals such as copper,
silver, and gold in the rocks, as well as
oil and natural gas.

These miners are digging for opals by hand.
It is hard and dangerous work.

Broken Hill in New South Wales is known as Silver City because of all its silver mines.

Opals are milky white precious stones. They sparkle with many different colors when held to the light.

In Queensland, there is enough rain to grow all kinds of fruit and vegetables. This farm grows pineapples.

Farming

Where there is enough water, farmers grow wheat, fruit, and vegetables. Only 70,000 people live and work in the dry Outback. Most of them raise cattle and sheep on huge farms called stations.

Farmers shear sheep for their wool.

The Outback

In the Outback, farms and small communities are very far apart. Life is very different for people living in these remote places.

The Flying Doctor Service began in Alice Springs in 1929. Alice Springs is in the middle of the Outback.

This boy lives a long way from a school, so he is learning geography over the radio.

Instead of going to school, children in the Outback take classes by radio. This means they may never see their teachers!
If people in the Outback are sick, the doctor comes to their house by plane or helicopter.

Australian Food

Because so many different nationalities live in Australia, many types of food are eaten—from spicy Chinese dishes to sweet Greek pastries. Australians enjoy eating outdoors and often cook steaks, sausages, and seafood on a barbecue.

The city of Melbourne has a large Greek population, so many shops sell Greek food.

Fresh fish is sold in markets all along the Australian coast.

Out and About

Australians play all kinds of sports.
They enjoy rugby, cricket, tennis, and golf.
Australia is also a great place for water sports.

Surfing is the most popular water sport in Australia.
The sea is warm and the waves can be very big.

This painting by an Aborigine shows a snake and a bandicoot (a kind of rat).

Many Aborigines are famous as artists. People go to see their paintings in caves and in art galleries.

Australians also enjoy going to the movies. Many successful films are made in Australia each year.

The popular movie *Babe* was made in Australia.

Festivals Old and New

Australia's National Day is January 26th.
On Australia Day there are big parties
all around the country.

People celebrate Australia Day with street parties
and carnivals.

This dragon is part of Chinese New Year celebrations in Sydney.

People from many different countries live in Australia. So festivals such as Chinese New Year and St Patrick's Day have become part of Australian life.

Visiting Australia

People visit Australia to see its amazing landscape, relax on its beautiful beaches, and experience the excitement and adventure of the Outback.

Uluru is a famous religious site for Aborigines.

Many tourists go diving in the Great Barrier Reef.

People also come to see Australia's native animals, such as koalas, kangaroos, and the duck-billed platypus.

Index

About This Book

The last decade of the 20th century has been marked by an explosion in communications technology. The effect of this revolution upon the young child should not be underestimated. The television set brings a cascade of ever-changing images from around the world into the home, but the information presented is only on the screen for a few moments before the program moves on to consider some other issue.

Instant pictures, instant information do not easily satisfy young children's emotional and intellectual needs. Young children take time to assimilate knowledge, to relate what they already know to ideas and information that are new.

The books in this series seek to provide snapshots of everyday life in countries in different parts of the world. The images have been selected to encourage the young reader to look, to question, to talk. Unlike the TV picture, each page can be studied for as long as is necessary and subsequently returned to as a point of reference. For example, school life in the Outback might be compared with their own, or a discussion might develop about the ways in which food is prepared and eaten in a country whose culture and customs are different from their own.

The comparison of similarity and difference is the recurring theme in each of the titles in this series. People in different lands are superficially different. Where they live (the climate and terrain) obviously shapes the sort of houses that are built, but people across the world need shelter; coins may look different, but in each country people use money.

At a time when the world seems to be shrinking, it is important for children to be given the opportunity to focus upon those things that are common to all the peoples of the world. By exploring the themes touched upon in the book, children will begin to appreciate that there are strands in the everyday life of human beings that are universal.